OPTIMUM LIVING
For Married and Singles

THE
CORNERSTONE
P U B L I S H I N G

DAVID O. KOLAWOLE

OPTIMUM LIVING

ISBN: 978-1-944652-50-0

Cornerstone Publishing
A Division Cornerstone Creativity Group LLC
Phone: +1(516) 547-4999
info@thecornerstonepublishers.com
www.thecornerstonepublishers.com

To order this book or for speaking engagement:
Dr. David O. Kolawole
+2348060380568;
davidakolawole@gmail.com
facebook: www.facebook.com/poweredplace
Instagram: @davidokolawole
twitter: @kolawole_gbenga

Printed in the United States of America

CONTENTS

FOREWORD

To every thing there is a season, and a time to every purpose under the heaven:
Ecclesiastes 3:1 (KJV)

He hath made every thing beautiful in his time: also he hath set the world in their heart, so that no man can find out the work that God maketh from the beginning to the end.
Ecclesiastes 3:11 (KJV)

I know that, whatsoever God doeth, it shall be for ever: nothing can be put to it, nor any thing taken from it: and God doeth it, that men should fear before him.
Ecclesiastes 3:14 (KJV)

Whenever I am asked to do a foreword for any book,I am always mindful of ensuring I have something specific to say before accepting such request.

Life is a school
Life is a journey
Life is a battlefield and
Life is a process etc

A lot of people are not able to get the most out of life because they do not realize the uniqueness of their lives journey especially the fact that life is a process with diverse times and season. Whenever you receive a promise from God,you will still need to go through a process before that promise can become a reality,many however do not know that so they give up while going through the process or they despise the process on the way to the promise. When you understand life and know what to do per time no matter where you stand,it will make your journey easy.

This book is all about helping you have that understanding and know what to do per time. The author has done a fine job here by helping to itemize and unveil specific factors you need to take on board to aid you journey in life.

I recommend this book to anyone who really wants to maximize their potentials and fulfill purpose.

Congrats pastor david for a job well done and for adding your quota to the array of rich resources to help humanity.

Olumide Emmanuel
International Speaker, Trainer and Author
Lagos, Nigeria

DEDICATION

This book is specifically dedicated to all
the past and present members of The
Triumphant Glorious Church Worldwide.

For over a decade, I have taught and Pastor
you with the word of life from the presence
of the Most high God with great results
following. You were my field oroducd training
and my Bank of experience.

To all those who have sat under my teachings
on marriage, singles life, entrepreneurship,
leadership, wealth creation, spiritual and
physical wellness and salvation; and are
producing results all around the world, thanks
for giving my ministry and calling a voice.

I love you all.

INTRODUCTION

We all must come to a realization that the demands for our time is a demand on our life; therefore, having and living our life to the fullest is what should be the goal of every one of us.

In this time and Era, the the demands for our attention comes from all directions; from carrier, family, friends, church and then, there are your own internal desires for fulfillment and significance. You feel the urge to leave a significant mark on the sand of time on this earth.

All of these and more needs to be taken cognisanc of; and then intelligently place in priorities. This is how to live life optimally. Life is a sentence of choices. You are going to make good choices -choices that will lead you to do great things and to make positive difference in life and in the lives of the people in your sphere of influence.

Knowing what really count and going head-long doing them - That is Optimum living.

CHAPTER ONE

THE BEAUTY OF RIGHT TIMES AND SEASONS

*"He hath made everything beautiful in his time….,
to everything there is a season, and a time to every
purpose under the heaven. A time to be born and a
time to die, a time to plant, a time to pluck up that
which is planted. a time to kill, and a time to heal;
a time to break down, and a time to build up; a
time to weep, and a time to laugh; a time to mourn,
and a time to dance; a time to cast away stones, and
a time to gather stones together, a time to embrace
and a time to refrain from embracing; A time to
get, and a time to lose; a time to keep, and a time
to cast away; a time to rend, and a time to sew; a
time to keep silence, and a time to speak; a time to
love, and a time to hate, a time of war, and a time
of peace; what profit hath he that worketh in that*

wherein he laboureth? I have seen the travail, which God hath given to the sons of men to be exercised in it. [Ecclesiastes 3:11, 1-10.]

It is certain that whatever we do, as long as we do it at the right time, it will emerge beautiful. In the scriptures above, we see King Solomon using contrasting issues to point our attention to a simple message of "appropriate timing" simply put; there is time allotment for everything that we wish to do in life. Therefore, if we do what we want to do in its right time, it becomes prosperous and makes our lives beautiful. The day is segregated and phased into morning, afternoon and night; and, time itself is divided into past, present and future; our lives are also in phases and in seasons. So if we do what we need to do at the right divide or season of our lives, our lives will turn out beautiful and well lived.

PAY ATTENTION TO YOUR LIFE NOW

We have lived on this earth and journeyed through life thus far, and before you know what's happening, we get old. There is actually not enough time for anyone of us to waste. Our time is so short that not an ounce of it is available for waste. If we do not do what we supposed to do now, we will have too much to deal with in the near future. But, if we deal with what we need to deal with now, by paying close attention to our lives at the time or seasons allotted to us, then a better livelihood can be guaranteed. Many of us are carrying into each other day, baggage that is not meant for the day, but was meant for days before. Some have even scheduled into tomorrow, the baggage that is not meant for tomorrow but for today. If we fail to do what we should do at the right and appropriate time, life then becomes difficult. Most things done out of season do not turn out well. If you must cultivate the quality life, you must start to do the right things at the right time.

LIFE IS IN PHASES AND MEN ARE IN SIZES

A good illustration of this is what a seasoned servant of God, apostle Paul said in 1 Corinthians 13:11 "when I was a child, I spoke as a child, I understood as a child, I thought as a child; but when I become a man, I put away childish things" Paul confirms that he had gone through phases in his life as well. He said that there were times that he was just a child, and all he could do was what a child was expected to do.

Whenever a child stops being a child and begin to act, or speak as an adult, assuming the position of an adult, that child will have to begin to deal with issues that he or she is not probably equipped to do nor cut-out to handle. Lots of people are already spent out by the time they are in the middle age. Because they started dealing with issues that their parents ought to have dealt with on their behalf. Since their parent failed to sort those things out, they now in their early stages of life, try to sort out what daddy and mummy should have done.

When you see a child who had to go through school and had to go to work at the same time, particularly in third world countries around the world; you then see reasons why many in such economies are not doing so well in their lives. Their attention is divided; it does not matter how well they tried to fair in their endeavors, something has been taken away from them. Divided focus rubs us of something that are more valuable than we know of. It has its consequence on our achievements and the results that we eventually have. Friend, we need to be closely aware of the times, phase and seasons that we are in so that we may pay attention and apply our heart to wisdom.

WHO AND WHERE ARE YOU?

It is very important that we understand the facts about times and seasons. This has to do with every area of our lives. It has to do with our academic, social and marital life. Your marital perspective is also affected by this concept, whether you are in marriage or out of it. No matter what class or phase you are in: single, married, divorced or widowed; It applies to us all.

In terms of marital status, you must first know where you fall in. according to Apostle Paul in 1 Corinthians 13:11, having a clear knowledge and understanding of your positional standing in life is very key and important, more importantly is; who are you?

That verse of scripture said, "When I was a child I spoke like a child, I understand like a child. You have to know who you are. If you are a man and a father you need the right and correct understanding to go with that status. Start being more responsible, provide for your family, provide security and create necessary time to spend with your spouse and children. Implant a good image of yourself in them at every opportunity you have to be around them.

You need to know where you stand at this point in time. Are you a married woman or a single lady. If you are a married woman, you should know the sacredness and the responsibility of the marriage union and what it means. You should not be found among irresponsible women who flirt around cheating on their spouse. You know that this lifestyle is not an option for you at all. If you are newly wed, the challenges that may face you may be the one that hinged around the fact that you and your partner are yet to come to terms with the facts that you both are now married. You want to still hangout with friends, and do what you want to do at the time you feel like doing it. Friend, you must come to term with reality. Your phase of life now is the marriage stage. You need to understand that in marriage; there is no more "I" or "me", but "we" and "us". there is no room for selfishness.

"Therefore will a man leave his mother and father and he will cleave unto his wife and the two shall become one flesh "Genesis 2:24." The body of the husband is no longer His own, it now belong to the wife. In like manner, the body of the wife no longer belongs to the wife but to the husband; both of them are one flesh. That is why the husband has every right, just as the wife also has every right to ask each other, "Where have you been?"

If you are single, you still have a right to your privacy and decide to do what you want to, as you want it done. If you have a date, the guy or lady(your boy or girl friend), does not have to know what you do or don't do. He or she does not have to know the places you have been to, because you are not yet married. You cannot say nor do anything that married people say and do to each other. You should not do things that married people do together. You are not in that season yet, there is time for everything; time to be single and time to be married. You could be dating each other but you must know the season that you are in. if you are not married, don't do what you are not expected to do. Don't say, "Since we are going to get married anyway, we can as well begin to sleep together". Show maturity and display understanding by not violating your seasons.

When you understand the particular phase of life that you are in, things work out accordingly. There is so much the scriptures have said to us in order to grow and maximize every season and phase of our lives.

In Philippians 2, Paul the apostle demonstrated a great understanding of who he was, where he was, and the future he saw in Christ, and what he taught of it all. He said when he had to abide by the law he was blameless. However, Paul concluded that for him to gain Christ, he had to lay aside everything he once gained; so that he may gain the excellence of the knowledge of Christ.

In essence, Paul was saying that, there are certain things we have to do today. There are other things that are meant for tomorrow. And, some certain things we have to do in the future. Friend, you should be able to compartmentalize your life into seasons and phases. Do the right thing in the right season. Back to our main verse in 1 Corinthians 13:11; Paul said; "I spoke as a child. I understand like a child, I thought like a child. But when I grew up, I put away every childish things!" he did what we all must do; grow up! We need to get mature in our understanding of times and seasons of our lives; and know the purpose of God for each of them seasons of our lives.

WHAT MATTERS TO YOU NOW?

The way a 20 years old single may act today is quite different from how a 35 year old single should act. when I was a child, I acted as child. When you were a 20 years old girl and boys came to ask you out, you could afford to say you don't want to go out with a particular kind of persons, but when you are a 35 year old woman, you should have an understanding of the time and season that you are in. this is when you need to tell yourself that your options today are not as many as the options you used to have when you were 20 years of age. your options are now fewer.

If you have a 10 months old baby and you give the baby your car keys, and say "my lovely child this is your car", what will happen the next minute is that the baby will throw the keys away and stuck its hand into its mouth right away. But, if you brought out a chocolate bar and stretch it to that child, the child will grab it and start to enjoy himself right away. This is so because, at that season of his life, that is what matters to him. That is why when you are 20 years of age, you can be choosy and selective about the guys that comes your way; if he is good looking, and if his outward appearance meets up with your standard. You may even want to know which schools he has attended and also check if his spoken English is Queen or American's; where he lives, whether he has 'six packs' and so on. If he is flashy enough, you say, "I love that guy", but when he is a guy that is not good looking enough, having low and humble background, not tasty enough in class, you say "I don't love that kind of guy".

But for a 35 years old woman, you don't like or dislike a guy because the guy is handsome or not. Your standards are not that of a young lady anymore but that of a matured woman. You want to find out more deeper and more important things about him. Your heart is not that of a baby but of a matured woman. The questions you ask are; "do you work? Or "what kind of job do you do?" "Do you have an accommodation of your own or do you scot with friends? Or "Are you ready to settle down in marriage now or is it latter? And "if its latter, how soon?" now your interest has suddenly changed because your understanding about life has changed, you are now more mature. Your heart content is no more what it used to be as when you were younger. That is why we can't present to a 35 year old woman the same message given to a 20 years old lady.

If I say to someone, "You can date for two or three years", that recommendation will certainly not be for somebody who is already 38. If you are at this age bracket, I believe you already have some level of maturity. At this phase of life, you don't need two or three years to know if somebody is good enough for you to get married to. In fact, at this juncture, six months is enough for courtship and you are good to get wedded. Why? Because your understanding is now different. Your discerning level is higher. At 35 you can smell a rat from afar because you may have experienced several heart breakage and so you recognize the traits when they show up. But an 18 or 19 years old lady won't know, that's why we can say to her, "hang-on a while more, and she can do that for another four to five years.

However that is not applicable to a 36 years old woman, she is no more a girl, she is a woman whose season of life is supposed to be the marriage season, not the dating season. Just like an 18 year old or 20 years old cannot meet somebody within six months and say "I know all about him I want to get married."

CHAPTER TWO

OPTIMIZE THE SEASON

⟡

There is an obvious need for you to optimize now because if you miss out on today you are going to pressurize your tomorrow. That is what we call "carry over." Don't carry baggage into your tomorrow that are supposed to be for today.

There are certain things we need to give maximum attention to right now. Ability to do these will save us of the need to worry in the near future.

Psalm 90:12 says ". . . teach us how to number our days, that we may apply our hearts unto wisdom." Or rather that we may gain a heart full of wisdom.

The psalmist suggests that wisdom is needed for you to be able to maximize the moment. You need a good deal of wisdom. We all do need a consciousness of the phase or season of life that we are in, this is gaining a heart of wisdom concerning the times. This will put you in touch with the reality of your moment, to help you understand that you are a married woman or a married man for instance; that no matter what happens or going on in your home, you have no option of changing spouses. In other words, wisdom helps you to understand what you have and what you don't have, what you need to do and what you don't have to do. It helps you to know the season that you are in and the options that comes with that season. Again, in marriage, wisdom teaches you to know that the option of divorce should not be considered. Because, God hates it. It is this wisdom that will enable you to know that at this point, you have moved into a season of tolerance, patience and intercession to make your marriage work.

For a 20 years old single person, wisdom also helps you to know that you have a wide range of options in front of you. Don't let the devil tell you that, once this guys comes, that's it and you begin to compromises God's standard for your life. At 20 or 21 years old, you must understand that you have a wide range of options, therefore, by wisdom, you should explore the options that you have and do that intelligently. Don't turn yourself into a whore as a girl, or into a Casanova as a boy.

One major challenge I have noticed in younger people is that some people, when they were 18, entered into a relationship with their immature hearts; They promised each other heaven and earth, and marriage when they had not know much about one another. At this season of their lives, they allow emotion alone to push them into marital commitments. They even go to the extent of taking oaths with each other in their innocent naivety. vowing and swearing to each other. As a result of their stupid decision, they suffer major emotional setbacks with hearts broken and shattered to bits and pieces. Some of them, never able to recover and pick their shattered lives together again, while a few others manage to learn a lesson, bounce back and move on with their brutally scarred hearts.

Why must you get married when you are not ready to get married? When you have the understanding of the right season of your life, things will go well and end better for you. The older folks had been thought that they have narrow options of marriage prone and cones. Instead of a 37 years old woman insisting that the name of the man she will marry must be peter or should start with p; at 37 years old, she should understand that it is not about the name, but about the man that bear the name. At this time of her life, a older woman or man don't insist that her husband to be must be this or his wife to be must be that. You don't have a wide range of potions anymore.

I think many people should stop being foolish and claiming to be acting in faith. At that age, you don't have too many options and you should be wise enough to recognize that.

COMMON SENSE

If you are the one who gave God the specifications of the kind of man or woman that you want, through the list that you wrote, either on paper or in your mind, then you should have the common sense to know that you are the one to make the prospect good. It's all coming from you and so, it all depends on you.

If you are connecting your list of choice to faith, that will rather be fake. Faith is holding God on His word, not holding Him 'on your own word.

If from the age of 22, you had that list of yours till you are now 36 and you still have not gotten your choice specification, don't you 'ever think that God had gone on a journey, it is high time you come to realize that your will is not God's will for your life after all.

Then, start asking for his wisdom to come upon your heart and make you of an understanding heart.

WHAT OTHER SEASON

The seasons of life are not only about marital relationships. There is need to have the understanding of the seasons that you are in concerning the other aspects of your life. Your career life, financial life, your business life, your political life and so on.

There are seasons of learning and there are seasons of earning. Season to develop your ideas and season to use the developed ideas to better your life and that of other people. There is a season to be a student and another of being a tutor. God makes all things beautiful in his own time with a heart full of wisdom, you can learn to put things in priority you need to begin to put everything about your life into the right perspective and the appropriate priority. Friend, get the right things into your life. start by being conscious of your thought life. Thinking right is critical and essential for a life that must be lived right. Remember, "As a man thinketh in his heart, so is he". Proverb 23: 7.

For example, you don't give your heart to who you want to get married to at tender age of 18, but rather to your studies. Don't you ever allow your mind to be filled with thoughts about marital relationship at this age, because this season is the right season for your study life. Face your studies with zeal, vigor and undivided attention. Once you finish your studies, there are more than enough time left to get your relationship right. Give your mind completely to what is important in every season of your life. It is the right thing to do. if you are a business person or a career person, put in all that you've got into what you do, so that you can become a major player in that field, therefore creating a niche for yourself in life.

ACT RIGHTLY

When it comes to finding a life partner, do it with all consciousness if it's the right time for it. Just as it is required of you to do the thinking, not God; so also it is important for you to act rightly at the right time. Don't you just go about your business and expect God to bring the man or the woman into your house. Remember the word of God that says, "He who findeth a wife has found a good thing." That tells you that the man and the woman are not just going to meet each other by accident, there is going to be a conscious and deliberate searching. You should know that when you are studying, the search could have been on. When you go for an interview, the search is also on. Whether at church, at work, at the bus stop or in the market. You are either searching or being searched for.

Hey, don't just search for your dream partner in your pastor's office, search for him or her in every where possible, except, of course in dead, ungodly places. By all means, if you're a wife, don't allow your husband to live your home without his wedding ring, because there are searchers out there everywhere! And, if you are a single lady, watch how you dress. If you have rings in your fingers the searcher who was supposed to find you might assume that you are engaged when you are not.

Act right because someone is searching and already eyeing you. Don't behave unreasonably either at home, on the street or at work, in the church in your community, your "Would be" spouse may not be there, but he or she has a cousin or a friend who is saying to his or herself, that, you may be the man or woman that will be a good match for his or her cousin ,friend or even nephew. That fellow may have been planning to link you guys up and see if things go well with you both. Therefore learn to act right in and out of season. Given no room for outburst of anger, give no room for arrogance and pride and give no room for mediocrity and laziness.

SPEAK RIGHTLY

"A man hath joy by the answer of his mouth and a word spoken in due season, how good is it!" -Proverbs 15:23. Self expression by words of mouth is a very good gift of God to man kinds. If well used and correctly marshalled, can be great blessing to a man's life and make his or her destiny glorious. Wisdom helps us to speak rightly; to express our heart in the right manner. At 38 years of age, a single woman or man's prayer should not be for God to give you the opportunity to go back to school to get a Ph.D. That should not be the big deal at that age and season of his or her life.

After the Ph.Ds, promotion at work, great rise in salary, latest cars and bigger finer house, what next. You need to understand that there is a time-frame for you to give birth to the next generation, and the next generation will give birth to the other generation and the covenant goes on. Let it not be dawn on you that you will soon become a disgrace to God's grace upon your life to your family and friends if you are still playing around at this age.

"He makes ALL THINGS beautiful in his time". When you go after the right thing at the right time, your life comes out with so much beauty. An 18 year old or 19 year old girl who comes back home with pregnancy is almost also a disgrace to her family. But a married woman who becomes pregnant has given the whole family a reason to rejoice and celebrate. Because she has done the right thing at the right time, in the right season. Right thing at the wrong season of life is out of place and a disgrace to timing.

DO YOU KNOW THE SEASON YOU ARE IN?

Friend, what season of life are you in right now. As a person, if I may ask, what season are you in by age, by what you are saying and how you are living your life. What are you pursuing? , what is your prayer content? What are your expectations? Are they right for the season that you are in now?

If you have the opportunity and the privileged to ask for whatever you want, what would be your request in your current season? And, if your request is granted, will it really make your life beautiful? Will it make you live a good, colorful, fruitful and fulfilled life? Will it ease the burden from your future or will it burden your future with yokes unbearably heavy? How are you able to optimize your living now?

Will you take advantage of the moment to maximize your living? What are you thinking about in contrast to what you should really be pondering about? Are you going to start setting your priorities correctly? Should you still be doing that same job or business, or are you supposed to make a change and take the big leap?

Isn't it time to own your own business? Start putting investments aside for your children instead of showering them with those expensive things? What should you be doing, thinking and seeing now? You are the only one who can, should and need to find answers that are peculiar to your own season at this time.

CHAPTER THREE

OPTIMIZE NOW!

Greatness is now; success is now and, now is the time for achievement. The now am talking about here is 'The moment'. There is actually no future without first giving the necessary consideration to the present moment. The key aspect of everything is always "The moment!" Because, "The past is in the tomb and the future is in the womb".

THE TIME IS NOW

"Thus saith the LORD, in an acceptance time have I heard thee, and in a day of salvation have I helped thee; and I will preserve thee and give thee for a covenant of the people, to establish the earth, to cause to inherit the desolate heritages" Isaiah 49:8.

All that we have to decisively optimize our living is "Now". It matters less if you are on the first, sixth or the last day on the calendar right now, what you must deal with is 'Now'. The time when God will help you is 'Now'. Now is your acceptable time. Now is when you will be protected, saved and be established. God's word did not promise the church His blessing for the future. The bible says that, "the set time to favour Zion is now!"

It becomes imperative for you now, to put your vision, dreams, ideas and aspirations together. Whosoever would not want their destiny disappointed, whosoever would not like to see his or her dreams fail, and would not wait to experience demotion and ridicules among equals in the near future; must focus all effort, strength and resources on "Now". If you lose focus on 'Now', your 'now' will become a carry over into your 'later'. That is why every one of us needs to continually pray, and ask our maker to help us be able to apply wisdom on what to do with those things that are in our past; and help teach us to apply wisdom in knowing what to do with those things that are in the future; most importantly, to help us to apply wisdom on what to do with our present, our now.

SHARE THE MOMENT WITH GOD

The biggest thing that can destabilize a man is when he begins to operate on a frequency he is not yet prepared for. Operating in another phase bigger or too much for his maturity. That is why it is important not to be in a hurry when you are on a walk with God in any area of your life.

A child of God that's on a life's journey with his maker needs lots of patience. There are times when you feel you are ready for something and God in His own understanding says; 'you are not due yet'. Forcing yourself into a closed door is wanting to break one or two bones in your body frame, that can't and won't be an experience any one of us will like to have in any situation, the word of God says to us to make our needs and requests known to God through prayers, supplications and patience. Don't you ever force your way into a closed door. Whenever you force open a door that God has not opened, what you are doing is that, you are at that same time, closing the doors that He has opened for you. Many time we are too fleshy or canal to known the perfect will of God for us in the now. Be prayerful. Never get married, get promotions, get jobs or do business through fleshy, diabolical or forceful means; it may, and will hurt your future. Carry God along on your way.

Optimizing your living today is not very possible until you know what your today has in store for you. What is your today in the agenda of God? You must know what God's programme is for your today. That is what will make you know where you fit into in the plan of God for the moment. When you have the understanding of the season that you are in, you will not jump ahead of God in anything you do or plan to do. Then, you will fit perfectly into His programme, plan and purpose for your life.

When you are the type that has learnt how to wait on God to know His plans, you will have developed the understanding that; sometimes the Lord, through His word will say "Be still", and in another situation, He says "Go forward". God is not a man – He will neither fail nor disappoint. He will always have an appropriate word for you that is presently relevant to the season but that word may not be appropriate for the next season. When the season changes, the word for the season also does, in most cases.

BE INSTANT IN SEASON

I am a family man with beautiful and wonderful children. Two of my four children are girls, they are just getting close to become teenagers. One of the two boys is already a teenager. With him I can discuss some things. But with the girls, it's not yet the time for my wife and I to discuss sex matters, because their minds are still too immature for such discuss. The senior boy is having his own swell time in some elementary sex education. Not only sex education, but some other matters too. There is the right time for everything under the heaven. Our children right now are at a stage where they are very inquisitive about everything, especially the youngest of them; not necessarily knowing what to do with the information he wants to get though.

My wife and I may not bother bombarding their young minds with what happens between a male and female just yet. But as they approach their teenage season of life, we have to start talking about sex and some other issues. How we do that is very simple. We must talk about the dangers of it, not the pleasures of it, at least for now. When they get into higher learning like the college or the university, we have to start changing what we say to them because we don't want to end-up fasting and praying for them to get married when the time comes.

When a child is in the university or other higher institution or levels of learning, that is the time the heart is receptive to things on relationship, career, finance and much more.

At elementary or high school phase of life, a child have no bills to pay; have no rents to pay for; there's no business nor job to care for or worry about. So, the one and only thing that should be important to that child is his or her studies and may be, his or her relationship, you know, the kinds of friends he or she is keeping at that time. Though you couldn't encourage that child about the opposite sex while in high school; at college or early levels in the university, you have to encourage them to begin to see good in the opposite sex. At this phase the children should begin to understand the both sides to; the good and the bad sides to an opposite sex acquaintance so that you can guide them in their relationship in the near future.

If you choose to say nothing about it, you may find out that when you send them off to the higher institution, they will find out things by themselves. The problem may now be that; their findings may not be the right ones, or from the right channels. Most parents have initially talked down on the opposite sex when the children, especially the girls are being raised up. They do it too much that the girls do not see anything good in the opposite sex even up to the time when they are due for marriage. By that time, to them, every man has become a suspect; including their own brothers and even their father. This should not be if you the parent do things that should be done in their right seasons.

When the times and seasons are changing, we should also change what we are saying, what we are doing and our perspectives to life. As a parent, what are your thoughts about developing your children? You need to be sensitive to their plights and situation at every stage. Be active all the way; as the season for our children changes, so must we change along with the times if we don't want to carry unnecessary baggage into both our future and theirs too. Let us brace up and begin to do what we need to do now. For a career parent, you have to know that the future of your child is more important than the money, the position or the accolades you get on that job. If you have children, the stage you are right now is the stage to find or create the time needed, and begin to pour wisdom into your children.

"My son, attend to my words; incline thine ear unto my sayings, let them not depart from thine eyes; keep them in the midst of thine heart. For they are life unto those that find them, and health to all their flesh." Proverbs 4:20 – 22.

From the verse of scriptures above, we understand that the words we hear and receive has great important to our destiny. When we are rightly tutored and raised by our parents, we come out better and grow up to become successful people. At every stage of life, the words that enters us and stay with us ends up transforming us. That is why it becomes very important to have time with our children pouring words of life into them.

Who is that person speaking with, to and into your children? Your, neighbors or the house help? Who is raising up your children? What are you pouring into your children, note that; the business will finish, the job will expire and the money made will be spent. The children are the tomorrow you have when you cannot work nor do business anymore.

I pray that when the future finally comes to you and you get to tomorrow, you will find rest, the peace of God be with you, and may you harvest joy unspeakable in the name of Jesus.

OPTIMIZE THE MOMENT DON'T HOLD BACK

While we continue to look on into the future, it's also important that we do not neglect today.

As believers, there are certain thing that we learnt and that were taught us when we were on our way growing up to this stage of our lives. There is a need to re-visit our Sunday School Lesson Notes, our sermon jotters and most importantly our Bible. You should have good understanding on every subject matters that will eventually matter to your future.

Learn about choosing of career, have good understanding about doing business and investment. Know something about economics, politics and sports. What are the things that are not in your life that you know should be in your life now and what is stopping you from having them into your life? The product of your 'now' is what becomes the future that you will eventually live in. Whatever you are doing now is the platform you will stand upon in your future to see even further. Don't lose today, don't disrespect the chances and the privileges of today, they are the parents that gives birth to tomorrow's opportunities. When you are focused on today, doing what you should be doing today and doing it well; you will eventually arrive at tomorrow and be glad you did. The seed of today is the fruit of tomorrow. What you do today is what you will meet up with tomorrow. The future starts now and tomorrow begin today. That is why it's being said that "whatever it is that's what doing at all, is what doing well".

The word of God also support the fact by telling us that; "Whatever your hands finds to do, do it with all your might". Ecclesiastes 9:10.

What are your aspirations? You need to know what are those things you want and then, set them up in order of priority. There's something the economics call "the scale of preference". This is a scale or a table that shows all of somebody's needs and wants in the order of their importance to the man who sets up the scale. You too must have one like that to help prioritize your desires or your wants in order, according to their importance or according to how pressing the needs are.

Are you planning to have a business of your own? How will you maximize the opportunities that God is giving you in order to have enough resources to start up your dream business? Do you want to get married soon? The question is what are you doing about it and what plans do you already have in plan? You have to know how to set your priorities right. Create needed time for your plan. You need to think, pray, plan and move into action to get your dreams come true. This means that you must do what you need to do right now, to get what you want to get tomorrow.

It's all about doing what you should do right now, today, this moment, not about what you did in the past. Not even about what you are going to do in the future. Do what you have to do now, do it right with the correct understanding. Be focus and be single minded until you get the answer right. Optimize the moment.

CHAPTER FOUR

GOD HAS A PLAN

Every believer in God should come to the understanding of the fact that God has a plan and a purpose for our lives. There is a reason why God made us, and a reason why we are alive and well is best known to Him – our maker. Life did not just happen, someone made it happen for a purpose. You are not a biological accident nor a genetic happenstance, but a deliberate formation and dispatchment to the earth.

Despite all your troubles, setbacks and challenges, you are still here standing strong and doing exploits. There is an obvious, deliberate intention in heaven for your life. That is why you survived and made it this far. Also, you should know that for that purpose of God for your life, there is an appointed time for fruition. Friend, at any particular time or season of your life, you must live with a consciousness that heaven has a programme for your life, just as He had plans for the people of old.

Prophet Jeremiah says; "Then the word of the Lord came unto me, saying; before I formed thee in the belly I knew thee; and before thou camest forth out of the womb I sanctified thee, and I ordained thee a prophet unto nations. Then said I; Ah, Lord God! Behold, I cannot speak: for I am a child.

But the Lord said unto me, say not, I am a child: for thou shall go to all that I shall send thee, and whatsoever I command thee thou shalt speak. Be not afraid at their faces: for I am with thee to deliver thee, saith the Lord" -Jeremiah 1:4 – 8.

What God was saying to Jeremiah was that "Irrespective of your person or personality, you are an instrument in my hand and I have a use, a genuine and profitable use for you, you are going to live your life to the glory of my holy name and power. I am very sure that Jeremiah was very surprised that day considering his age, environment and the prevalent circumstance surrounding him at that particular time. He could not believe he had a place in the programme of God for that moment. That should pass a message to you: there is something for everyone of us in God.

All you need to do is to find out what it is. When you understand it you can then position yourself on time to fulfill that purpose. Now you know what's in store for you. It is to bless you and display the glory of God through you, don't accept anything short of that from the devil.

Maybe you have missed it in the past or goofed once or twice before, but I want you to know that God has not given up on you yet. God has in his hand, not just second, third or fourth chances, but He certainly gives more chances than you can ever imagine. One may miss it over and over again, but because of God's programme for your life, you will keep bouncing back again and again. Your maker will keep showing you mercy once and again until grace lifts you up.

The thing is, God would not give up on you neither will He give up on your dreams, If you won't as well. He never stops until His purpose is fully accomplished and His very will is done.

Remember, your past is not as important to God as your present. When God wants to bless you He bless you now. If He gives you a promise for the future, He begins to work on you now, so that you can come into His promise for the future. The bible says that, the time to favour you and I is now. The time for your favour is never in the past neither is it going to be in the future. It is in the "Now".

Here this, "Thou shall arise and have mercy upon Zion: for the time to favour her, yea, the set time is come (the set time is Now!). Psalm 102:13.

Take note that heaven's focus is not on who you used to be, but on who you are right now. What you do now is more important to the ultimate purpose of God's counsel in your life. The favour and blessings of God are in the now, that is why it become highly important that you connect yourself with His original purpose for your life now. That and more is the key to your fulfillment in life and destiny.

Begin to have the right feelings. Feel what God is saying about your life. Get yourself to conform with what His intentions are concerning your assignments here on earth. Even when you feel inadequate sometimes, you will need to go beyond that inadequate feelings into the very voice of God that is calling out to you now?

MANAGING PEOPLE

If you must have an optimum living, you have to do some things necessary for this very time space that you are given now. One of the things you must know how to handle now is, dealing with people. There are lots of people that are connected to your destiny assignment; and you must learn how to manage your relationship with them, people that come and go in and out of our lives are very important to either the making or the breaking of our lives. Managing people requires the absolute wisdom of God and personal discipline. Many times you have to be strong to make quality decisions concerning the people that are related to your life. The people that surrounds your life are the ones that determines how your life will turnout. That is why knowing the right ways to dealing, handling or relating with them has direct correlation to your purpose and existence here on planet earth.

There are times that you need to take decisions

that are somehow strict and tough. You should know when to say, 'yes' and also when to say 'no'. some people are only good for yesterday; they appear to have served the purpose for which they are connected to you, let them go! Holding on to such people may lead to crippling the limbs of your progress or slowing it down. Yes, they were good to you and for your life's assignment yesterday, but their time has simply expired. No matter how much you still want them to be a part of your life, they won't because; they are simply done!

Imagine you are in a bus heading towards a particular destination with other people, you are meant to alight at a specific bus-stop 'A', meanwhile, the driver did not stop, instead, he heads towards bus-stop 'B' while every other person might be enjoying the ride, you won't because you know that you are supposed to have been out as far as that trip is concerned, both psychologically, emotionally and otherwise, you are don!

Likewise, with the people in and around your life, you need to realize and accept this hard reality, so that you can move forward as it has to do with God's agenda for your life.

As it is, we all need the right people around our lives. You need people who are excited about what God is doing with you and with your dreams. Those people who are excited and jubilant about what God is doing about your vision, mission and pursuit in life, those who see God's hand upon your life and celebrate. These are the kinds of people you should keep or allow to stay around your life. When you begin to notice fault finders who are always talking about the things you are not doing well, those who say, you did this and you did that with no just evidence; it might be that their time is already up. Let them off the boat of your life. Your relationship by destiny is already expired.

Remember, one Jonah on a boat is enough to sink a whole boat. May God help you if you are a 'man-pleaser'. Men pleasers has a very terrible weakness; instead of focusing on the purpose of God for their lives, they rather focused on how to get into the good-book of people; instead of getting on with what they are called to do, they are seeking to please people. This habit is a surest way to missing out on the will or intention of God for one's life. Every person who must be a 'man of purpose' has to perfect the art of human management. Yes, there are times to give listening hears, times to give lending hands, times to be gentle and easy and times to be a little strict, hard or harsh, times to be friendly and time to become unfriendly.

If you are an employer, it is good that you care for your staff, it may be true that many of them may not be used to being cared for, however, you still have to care for them very well.

SOW THE SEED NOW

When the bible talks about a time to lose, some people in their religious mindset would say God forbid, I will not lose anything in my life'. But the thing is, we have to trust the scriptures. You have to be in tune with God.

If you are a businessman, you must understand that, it is not every business transaction that you win. In the business world, you win some and you lose some. That is exactly what the bible is talking about when it says, a time to lose. There are some certain things that you will intentionally let go of. It is called seeding. It is the seed for the future harvest, and seed is always smaller compared to the harvest.

'While the earth remaineth, seedtime and harvest and cold and heat, and summer and winter, and day and night shall not cease.-Genesis 8:22.

According to the words of the scripture above, everything in life is subject to this particular order of see-time and harvest-time. Whosoever will not seed cannot, and should not harvest. Whatsoever you want out of life, there has to be a see-time for the harvest that you want. There will be times when all you will have to do is to keep making inputs. There will also be times when all you will be experiencing is income, which is also called, 'the harvest'.

Whosoever wants love should sow love. If money is what you want, then sow money. Is it joy that you want, sow the seed. There is a seed in your hand for the result you wish to see around you, sow that seed. You know, the thing is, when you are parting with your seeds, it looks like you are losing something. When you have to make some financial inputs, it looks like you are losing the money. But, you should remember and keep it in your heart that; you are doing what you are doing because you have an expectation.

FINANCIAL EXPECTATIONS

Sowing financial seeds like, the first fruits, the miracle seeds, tithing, project investments in the church, may sometimes feel difficult; it may feel like you are losing the money. On the contrary, you are setting your harvest in motion. Because, if you go through 'a time to lose', you will arrive at 'a time to gain'.

There is a time for everything under the sun. if you do the right thing today, you don't have to worry about what you did wrong yesterday. It is possible that you made some mistakes yesterday or some people disappointed you yesterday, but that's all in the past. What matters most is what you are going to do now.

CHAPTER FIVE

TOMORROW IS GUARANTEED

Friend, your seed today is your tomorrow's guarantee. What you do with today is what you live with tomorrow. If you are faithful with little, more will be committed into your hands. If you are not faithful with little, God has no obligation to commit more to you. If you cannot do something spectacular with today, why should God guarantee any tomorrow? Don't waste today, else tomorrow won't wait for you.

God has given you 24 hours in a day. Have you maximized the 24 hours? Have you justified 6 out of the 24? or 20 out of 24? How are you going to account for the other remaining four? He gave you 24. When you begin to say you don't care about the whole day, He will begin to ask you why he should give the next two months, or the next one year? It's good sometime to reason together with God (Isaiah 1:18).

I read the account of a pastor friend's son, who came back from school with so much excitement, and said, 'Dad, I got 12 over 15 in my spelling assignment. My friend ask his son, 'Am I supposed to throw you a party for that? 'The boy said, 'Dad, but I tried.' My friend said yes you did, but I think I paid for the whole 15, I didn't pay for 12! My friend needed to know what happened to 'Excellent' and 'very good' he needed to know what happen to 15 over 15. He needed his son to account for the remaining 3 that were Paid for!

A lot of people are celebrating average, and they become aggrieved when they are asked to account for the remaining half. The time has come for you to maximize what you have been given. Optimize your living with what you are given. Pick up yourself and come to realize that what you have is what you have. You will make the best of what you have now when it's down on you that, what you have is exactly what others also have; one life, one day, 24 hours a day, seven days a week; four weeks a month and 12 months a year.

The failure of yesterday should not deny you of the opportunities of today. What you did or didn't do, what happened or didn't happened for you yesterday shouldn't be a hindrance to your progress today. 'Now' is critical to your 'later'. The choices you make today will determine the quality of life you live tomorrow. If you observe the wind, you will not sow. Your actions or inactions of today will count for tomorrow. Are you an employee today? Don't just go to that office to mark the register; whatever you pick or learn on the job now could have impact on your future endeavors, like Bishop Jakes says in his book 'maximize the moment'.

The race is indeed not to the swift, the battle is certainly not to the strong, but 'time' and chance (opportunities) happens to them all. Whatever you do with your time and the opportunities that come your way will determine how optimal your living will be, in terms of your accomplishments and fulfillments.

'Now', is a miracle! Don't waste your now when it shows up. Your 'now' moments are very important to your accomplishments in life. If you have not yet experienced 'now' moments in your life, I assure you that it does shows up for you every day you wake up to see a brand new day. It does shows up for me too, on daily basis.

God has hidden our breakthroughs in our 'now'. Remember He said, 'the time to favour Zion is now, now is so significant to our lives, that we can't afford to disregard now. All that we must do and keep doing is to place and keep placing the right value on our 'now'.

GRAB HOLD OF YOUR CHANCE

Jesus was once passing through the city of Jericho; Bartimaeus the blind was along the roadside. Though blind, but heard from the crowd that Jesus was passing by, there and then, he knew it was his 'time', his 'chance' and his 'moment' yes, it was not very easy and cheap, people tried to shout him down. They said "He has already passed and gone! Another time and chance will come for you, Jesus always passed through here anyway!" They said, "maybe next week or tomorrow, then you can get his attention," but Bartimaeus knew that his moment was 'now' and not tomorrow nor next week. He decided not to allow his own opportunity slip away regardless of what the people were saying. He just couldn't take being blind for one more day.

When Jesus finally called him, after his insistent shouts: the bible says he threw away his garment, which represented his troubles, pains, disappointments and setbacks of the past. He knew another week was not good enough for him in that dilapidated state, while he has now! He decided to optimize his living by grabbing hold of his now. He freed himself of his excuses, bitterness and unforgiveness, seized the moment and got his miracle. What Bartimaeus did was what God expects of all of us. To free ourselves of all our excuses and go after the opportunities around us now!

MAKE CHOICES – TAKE DECISION

One thing that can keep you away from the miracle that are available for you now, is when you are an indecisive person. Many are so undecided about what to do now. Indecision about the choices you need to make; indecision about the things you should have done and indecision about the actions that you need to take. Unfortunately, many are holding back. They are into prolonged fasting and prayers when all they are expected to do was to take steps and make decisions. The place of prayer must never be underrated, yes, but prayer cannot be an alternative to decision making and making choices that one need to make.

God makes everything beautiful in its own time, that is prayer inclusive. However, every time is not a time for prayer. Therefore, you have to know when to pray about matters and when to act on the matter.

One decision you should always be ready to make is risk taking. The test of your faith in god is your ability to take risks, believing God to see you through. There is an element of faith in walking in faith. While holding onto, and running with what God has commanded you to do, you must realize what it means to take risks. Take that risk, do whatever God is leading you to do by faith, He will always show up in the journey.

Sometimes when you are involved in business transactions, it may not always look the outcome you prayed for, but you have to take steps.

Sometimes you lose, and many times you win. However it turns out, God will always show up to make it up for you. Because what God is doing for you to have confidence in his leading of you. Don't be over protective, and don't be too defensive, it might make you lose out of the very best of God for your life. You know, when God leads, He leads you into the wilderness straight through Jericho and Jordan into your promised land. Make decisions, make choices, take risk and at the end, you will win.

TIME MANAGEMENT

"To everything there is a season, and a time to every purpose under the heaven: A time to be born, a time to die; a time to plant, and a time to pluck up that which is planted, A time to kill, and a time to heal; a time to break down, and a time to build up; A time to weep, a time to laugh; a time to mourn, and a time to dance; A time to cast away stones, and a time to gather stones together; a time to embrace, and a time to refrain from embracing; A time to get, and a time to lose; a time to keep, and a time to cast away; A time to rend, and a time to sew; a time to keep silence, and a time to speak; A time to love, and a time to hate; a time of war, and a time of peace... He hath made everything

beautiful in his time; also he hath set the world in their heart, so that no man can find out the work that God maketh from the beginning to the end. I know that there is no good in them, but for a man to rejoice, and to do good in his life. Ecclesiastes 3:1-12.

If I may ask, have you achieved what you set out to do this particular time of the year? Did you make use of all chances that you got? Many opportunities that came your way from the beginning of this year, which many people were not privileged to have, how did you use them? What have you done with your life all these years up till now? Until you wake up daily and set out to do something tangible with your life, you would not be able to give a proper account of your entire life to this point- your time is your life. Time is life!

Set goals. This will help you to measure how well you are doing in every area of your life. If you are an employer, it is important that you set a goal of having good relationship with your employees. If you are a businessman, you have to set a goal for your relationship with your clients. In the business world, customer is king; the customer is always right! The clients are the boss. This is so because if they don't patronize you, you won't have a business to oversee.

Through your relationship with God, your relationship with co-workers and your relationship with your customers, you will decide what you want and where you are going each year, each quarters and each month in your life and business. God has a scheduled assignment already planned out for your life per time. You will not miss out of his divine purpose for your life in the mighty name of Jesus.

You may not know how much money God wants to give you in the next quarters of the year, but you must know that God is taking you out of poverty, out of debts and out of all forms of lack. It is important that you have a sense of where you are going. God cannot, and will not take you from were you are and put you in poverty. Having the vision of your future will make you begin to develop the required passion for your destination. By so doing, you will begin to get tired of where you are and getting excitement of where you need to be. It is the passion for where you want to go that tells everyone around you that you are really tired of where you used to be.

Those who do not have any destination in sight will be comfortable with their present location. It is like two people driving in a highway. When one person is doing pleasure driving, going for a pleasure ride, and the other on purposeful driving, going to a definite destination. The man on a pleasure ride does not have a limited time to get off the road. But the man with a defined destination, driving on the fast lane having a definite time to get off the highway to arrive at his destination. While one is being overtaking, the other one is doing the overtaking. This suggest the reason while someone won to Christ or brought to church gets in and become more receptive of the word of God than someone who had always been in church. That new person in the church has a passion for what is being taught in the church, and his or her passion has become noticeable and led to his/her steady prayers and growth in the things of God. Friend you must have the passion required for your future. When you are making your decision for your destination, it has to be a SMART one.

That means Specific, Measurable, Achievable, Realistic and Time –Specific decisions (Smart). In no time, your vision will become a reality.

YOU NEED A MIND RENEWAL

"And be not conformed to this world: but be ye transformed by the renewing of your mind, that ye may prove what is that good and acceptable and perfect will of God. –Romans 12:2.

To get away from where you used to be to where you need to be, you must begin to change your way of thinking and the way you are used to see things. Your old ideology has to be changed and your beliefs has to be transformed. Your ideology about the economy, about finance and about people must be changed to make it align with God's own ideology, God's word. Tell yourself that you can make it, that you are creative and that you bare blessing to your world. God sees you as a creative, innovative and productive personality. Do not see yourself otherwise.

With this confidence, go out there and find what your world needs and become the answer to their needs. Be the solution to the confusions that be. It's your time, make it count. Optimize your living!

PRAYERS FOR YOU

1. Thank the Lord for the grace to be committed to your purpose.
2. Thank the Lord for giving you a reason to laugh in life.
3. Pray for godly attitude that will influence other people positively.
4. Ask the Lord for positive attitude inside, that will change the outside.
5. Receive strength and encouragement and help from Holy Spirit.
6. Ask the Lord to anoint your eyes to see how your problem can be settled.
7. Pray that the Lord will use you as light in the darkness of this world.
8. Ask the Lord to uproot the negatives of the past from your life.
9. Ask that your destiny be not hindered by your past misfortunes.
10. Pray for a heart that is single-minded in serving the Lord.
11. In times of discouragement, pray that your face will look to God.
12. Pray to stay within the revealed plan of God for your life.
13. Pray to break every limitation that is stopping you from succeeding.

14. Pray to cancel every satanic attack of intimidation by the blood.
15. Pray for the grace to have single minded commitment to God.
16. Ask the Lord to help you live a life that is full of testimonies.
17. Pray that your life will be a source of light to these in darkness.
18. Pray that God gives you power to live a life that glorifies Him.
19. Reject every trace of hypocrisy that might be found in you.
20. Reject all un-forgiveness, repent and ask God to forgive you.
21. Pray that you will be filled with the God-kind of affections.
22. Pray for grace to set your heart on heavenly things.
23. Thank the Lord for the heart that desires to serve Him.
24. Pray for the heart of genuine compassion towards the unsaved.
25. Ask the Lord for the grace to prefer others before yourself and that nothing hinders the flow of your joy .Praise God Hallelujah!

ABOUT THE AUTHORS

David O. Kolawole is a much sought after insightful teacher, preacher, motivational speaker and author of several books on excellent leadership, successful living, Business exploits and Entrepreneurship. He is a full gospel Apostle with prophetic grace. The president of David Kolawole Ministry International (DAKOLMINT), the president of Eagle's Wings International, the founder and senior pastor of the Triumphant Glorious Church International (TGC Int.), The president of Dominion Bible Institute, Lagos-Nigeria (DOBLIN), The Director of the ministry's mission school (Medalland International Schools) also in Lagos Nigeria.

He is married to Precious Omolola Kolawole who pastors with him, she is the president of the "Zion Daughters International", an organization that brings hope, healing and empowerment to homes, women and children. She is an author and proprietor of Medalland International

Schools. They live in Lagos –Nigeria with their four wonderful children (two boys and two girls); David Adedamola, Precious Adebolanle, Adedolapo Delight and Olugbenga Praise.

ABOUT THE BOOKS

This is a book that will not allow you to settle for less than you are capable of you must not be allowed to be less than God wants you to be. This teaches ageless biblical principles that reveal the keys to personal success available to everyone of us, if we know where to look, what to do and when to do them. Every moment of the days of our lives are blessed and loaded with opportunities.

By the wisdom package in this book, you will; Release yourself from damaging relationships Have courage to face and conquer past failures Discover and utilize God-given grace on your life to its fullest. Set goals, develop strategies to accomplish your purpose in life.

Raise godly children, nurture a great family and ultimately optimize your living here on Earth!

Other Books By the Author:

- A WILL TO SUCCEED
- BE FREE AND FLY

- THE PROGRESSIVE DESTINY
- MY WORLD IS BEAUTIFUL
- NOT ANY MORE AFFLICTED
- ACHIEVING SUCCESS
- THE BLISSFUL SINGLE

TO CONTACT THE AUTHOR:

DR. DAVID O. KOLAWOLE
+2348060380568   davidakolawole@gmail.com
https://web.facebook.com/poweredplace
Instagram: @davidokolawole
twitter: @kolawole_gbenga